Old Ochiltree
Alex F. Young

Mill Street looking to Main Street around 1900, showing the renovated Cross. The building on Mauchline Road corner, to the right, was built in 1897 by New Cumnock born grocer John Jamieson Probert (1849-1944) The shop entrance was on the corner and his home above. Probert was Registrar of births, deaths and marriages from 1876 until 1935. In July 1967, the driver of a brewer's lorry from Ayr, heading for Catrine, took the right fork for Cumnock, realised his mistake, stopped, reversed, and collided with the pillar, breaking it into three pieces. It was repaired, although the joins are still visible, and was restored in 1977 by Cumnock and Doon Valley Council to mark the Silver Jubilee of Queen Elizabeth II.

© Alex F. Young, 2012.
First published in the United Kingdom, 2012,
by Stenlake Publishing Ltd.
Telephone: 01290 551122
www.stenlake.co.uk

ISBN 9781840336023

The publishers regret that they cannot supply copies of any pictures featured in this book

Printed by
P2D Books, 1 Newlands Rd, Westoning, Bedford MK45 5LD

Acknowledgements

Gary Eastman of Bierrum International, the Hon. Curator of the Ayrshire Yeomanry Museum, Hugh Brown, James Brown, Pamela Lockie, Isabel Montgomery, Ian Hope of Hope Homes, and Sheila Struthers.

Left: The Cross, around 1895, with William Gilmour (on the left) and William Wyllie. Gilmour was born in 1880 to Annie Gilmour who, later that same year, married William Smith, from Crosshill, Ayrshire. Wyllie was a horse dealer who at this time was living in Manse Road. He died in Burnock Street in August 1896. In August 1872 he had been prosecuted, at the instance of the Glasgow Society for the Prevention of Cruelty to Animals, having left a horse with a broken leg to suffer needlessly, and was fined 30/- or 30 days imprisonment. Until 1884, when he was sequestrated, he rented the 70 acre Slatehole Farm, off the Ochiltree to Mauchline road, dealing in horses.

A pillar, marking the Cross, stood here as early as 1513, but this one probably dates from 1836, and shows the need for the renovation work of 1897 which marked the Jubilee of Queen Victoria. The Glenfield & Kennedy of Kilmarnock pillar fountain was replaced with a new design at a cost of 45/-.

Introduction

Blaeu's *Atlas of Scotland*, published in 1654, shows 'Uchiltree Castle' which would have had a small supporting community. The 1792 *Statistical Account of Scotland* describes the parish (an area of 30 square miles) but gives little detail of the village. Of the 220 families in the parish, 67 lived in the village. By 1832, when John Thomson surveyed his *Atlas of Scotland*, the area around The Cross was developing.

Pigot & Co.'s *Commercial Directory of Scotland* (1837), describes Ochiltree as 'a small but pleasant village', and lists the shopkeepers and traders. There are grocers, bakers, shoe-makers, blacksmiths and cartwrights, but also shearing hook manufacturers (Hector Walker and James Brown) – with a market far and wide across the country, a fishing rod maker (Mungo Pedden), a snuff box maker (Alexander Murdoch) and two snuff box painters (Matthew Colville and David Hitchinson). Other employment was found on the farms and the roads.

The coming of the railway in the 1870s brought work – from its building to its operation – and the opening of the Barony Colliery in 1910 brought even more. Ochiltree had no miners' rows, but the increase in workforce spurred Ayr County Council to build the houses in Broom Crescent and Mill Street in the 1930s. The sinking of Killoch Colliery in 1953 further stretched the availability of housing. The collieries and their jobs are now gone, but house building goes on, as buyers seek the open air of the Ayrshire countryside.

Opposite: General Sir Charles Fergusson (1865-1951), 7th Baronet of Kilkerran and Lord Lieutenant of Ayrshire, addressing the gathering at the unveiling of the war memorial on Sunday 1st October 1922. Earlier, a procession consisting of the firing party and buglers, Auchinleck Pipe Band, Sir Charles, James Brown, M.P., Mr Adam W. Montgomerie of Lessnessock, the Rev. Neil Mackay (parish minister from 1880 until 1930), Col. William Thomas Reginald Houldsworth (1874-1960) and Col. J. D. Boswell and Major J. C. Kennedy, both of the Ayrshire Yeomanry, had marched from the Cross to the parish church for a service, before returning to unveil the monument then draped with the Union flag. A volley of three shots was fired and the buglers sounded the 'Last Post'.

Right: In his speech at the unveiling service James Brown (1862-1939), the Labour Party's Member of Parliament for South Ayrshire in 1918-1931 and 1935-1939, quoted a line from John McCrae's poem 'In Flanders Fields' – *though poppies grow in Flanders fields*, but it took time for the poppy to be adopted as a universal symbol of the Armistice. This photograph was taken after the unveiling service, hence the 'floral' tributes. Of the 38 men commemorated that day, all but one (Artificer James Hall of the Royal Navy) were army and variously served with the Royal Enniskilling Fusiliers, the Royal Scots Fusiliers, the Highland Light Infantry, the Ayrshire Yeomanry, the Royal Highlanders (Black Watch), the Machine Gun Corps, the Royal Field Artillery, the Royal Army Ordnance Corps and three Commonwealth regiments. The Second World War caused eight more names to be added.

Main Street in the 1940s, with Ayr Road to the left at the war memorial. On the right was the Ochiltree branch of Auchinleck Co-operative Society which opened in 1899. The blond sandstone building comprised the shop and four houses, one for the grocer and the others rented and was owned by John Gemmell (1831-1886) of Glencairn Cottage, Main Street and then his wife Sarah Colville or Gemmell who died in 1901, aged 69 years. The Co-op then had a new landlord, the saddler, John Purdie, but they bought the premises in the 1920s. Main Street rises steeply from this junction, hence 'Smiddy Brae' or 'Weir's Brae' after the blacksmith John Weir, whose former premises stand on the left of the picture. At this time the smiddy, with its petrol pump, to the left of the memorial, was occupied by William McCurdy but still owned by the Weir family. In the days when road surfaces were much poorer than today, this was an obstacle for heavily-laden carts and led to the opening of Ayr Road in the late 1830s.

Ayr Road from the war memorial to the Free Church, and Blackbush Cottage on the horizon. On the left, a Buttercup Dairy Company's van from Cumnock – one of 250 branches across Scotland and the north of England – is making a delivery. Over the years, the war memorial, like the Cross, was struck by vehicles and increasing traffic volume was thought a danger to Armistice Day services. The opening of the new community centre on Main Street in March 1972 presented a possible site, but the following year the council acquired the decrepit Free Church and had it demolished. Some of its stone ended up re-enforcing the banks of the mill lade at the sawmill and the war memorial moved to its present site. The Rev. John Heron (parish minister, 1971-1979) conducted the dedication service on Sunday 9th September 1973.

The Free Church on Ayr Road with, on the left, Doctors Road giving a sight of the Established Church on Main Street. At the Disruption – over the rights of 'parish heritors' to appoint the parish minister – in May 1843, 121 ministers and their congregations broke away and formed the Free Church of Scotland. Support for the separation was not as strong in Ochiltree as elsewhere, but sufficient enough to form a new congregation. The building was inaugurated on Sunday 8th March 1846 by the Rev. Thomas Guthrie (1803-1873), leader of the Free Church of Scotland, who was commemorated by the unveiling of a statue on Edinburgh's Princes Street in 1910. Its capacity of 500 was greatly exceeded for this first service, the collection helping towards the building cost debt of £125. The first minister was Joseph Patrick (1814-1871), whose son, David (1849-1914), was head of W & R Chambers, the Edinburgh publisher, and responsible for their *Biographical Dictionary*. The two churches united in 1929, this becoming the South Church, with the established church being the North, but the costs of running both were unsustainable, and in 1934 the congregation was dissolved. During the Second World War the church was commandeered by the War Department as a centre for Land Army girls and the Home Guard under the command of William Watson, the public assistance officer in Burnock Street. The fate of the five cwt, 30 inch, bell, cast by the Gorbals Bell Foundry of Glasgow and donated by John Bryden, who died in March 1845, aged 93 years, is not known.

Main Street in 1907 looking from Smiddy Brae to the Cross, at the junction of Mill Street and Burnock Street. The Auchinleck Co-operative Society is awaiting its new shopfront, and the corner onto Ayr Road awaiting the coming – and going – of the war memorial.

The view east down Main Street, flanked by the cottage at no. 52 on the left and on the right by the thatched house where the semi-detached block (nos. 29 & 31) of ex-local authority houses now stand.

Smiddy Brae in the late 1950s or early 1960s when, as the roofless cottage on the left, beside Willowbank, shows, the village was at a low point. The shell was subsequently demolished and new buildings erected at the rear.

Main Street, looking west, with the whitewashed Star Inn (possibly, at this time occupied by John Crichton Stewart) on the left, and the church belfry reaching above the roofline on the right.

The foundation stone of the simple, Gothic style, parish church on Main Street, was laid on 16th May 1789, by James Boswell (1740-1795), 9th Laird of Auchinleck and biographer of the poet and essayist Samuel Johnson, and the Right Honourable Elizabeth, Countess Dowager of Glencairn (1725-1801). The building work was left to the local mason, Hugh Morton. The original church, dating back to the 12th century, was located in what is now the old graveyard in Mill Street. The Rev. David Grant (*Davie Bluster* in the Robert Burns poem *The Kirk's Alarm*) served as minister from 1786 until his death in July 1791. The quality of Hugh Morton's work can be questioned, for by 1896 the building was in a dangerous state of disrepair. James Pettigrew Wilson of Polquhairn's objection to the renovation work was overruled by Ayr Presbytery, and the Edinburgh architects John More Dick Peddie and George Washington Browne saw the work through – the church re-opening on 11th December 1898. Through the munificence of James Angus of Ochiltree House, a hall was built in 1908 and extended in 1958, at which time the wall to the right of Hollybank Cottage was demolished to give vehicular access to it. Around 1942, the two stained glass windows by the Edinburgh artist Stephen Adam (1848-1910) were brought from the Free Church and installed on either side of the pulpit. The windows are dedicated to John (1785-1875) and Jean (Mearns) Lammie (1789-1868), and to Alexander (1791-1882) and Agnes Gregg (1795-1864), and were commissioned by their daughter Jean Gregg and her husband George Lammie.

Left: The Rev. David P. Leishman conducting a Harvest Thanksgiving service in the parish church. A native of Lanarkshire's Dalserf, he was educated at Larkhall Academy and then trained as a mining engineer before enrolling and graduating from Glasgow University in 1933 with a Master of Arts degree. Three more years of study won him a Bachelor of Divinity degree and he was licensed by the Presbytery of Hamilton in 1936. After three years at Galashiels he translated to Bargrennan in Wigtownshire from where, in August 1945, he came to Ochiltree, succeeding the Rev. Angus MacLeod, as the parish's twentieth minister. In 1952 he returned to the Borders, serving the congregation of St. Boswells Parish Church until his retiral in 1973. He died at Durisdeer, Dumfriesshire in 1989, aged 84 years.

Opposite: Main Street from the Broom Crescent junction, on the left, to the 1906 building at the junction with Ayr road. The vacant plot on the left now has a bus shelter, whilst the cottages on the right were swept away to build the present school. Seated on the stone outside his cottage is the carter John Peden.

Broom Crescent running down to Main Street, in the late 1950s, with the Barony Power Station on the horizon – today's blot is the Egger plant, opened in 1998. In the late 1930s Ayr County Council acquired land across its area for new housing, including Broom Crescent and Mill Street, in Ochiltree. In this photograph, those houses built in the 1930s are flanked by the post-war buildings, partly in the view. The last block on the right – nos. 9 to 15 – were occupied, from the first week in June 1938 by John Blair, Peter Bryne, Thomas Woods and John Miller, each with his family. Building resumed after the Second World War, taking the Crescent back onto Main Street, with Gallowlea Avenue, to which was later added Stewart Avenue, Poole Avenue and Douglas Brown Avenue.

The new school was opened by Mrs. David W. Shaw of Ayr (who was also responsible for the convalescent home) in August 1909. The architect Alexander Caldwell Thomson (1873-1925) of Ayr designed it to guidelines by the Scotch Education Department (he also designed the Claud Hamilton Memorial Hall in Coylton, Sinclairston School, Auchinleck School and Mauchline's war memorial). The entrances, girls on the left and boys on the right, led into a central hall with two classrooms on either side. The masonry work, Ballochmyle sandstone, was by Messrs. Kerr and Morton of Ochiltree and the joiner was John Dalziel of Auchinleck. By the following week 190 pupils, still under the guidance of headmaster, Mr. Archibald Andrew, would be at their desks. He retired in July 1915 and died at his home at 2 Maybole Road, Ayr in 1932, aged 81 years. The opening of the new school in 1976, reduced the 'old school' to a local authority store until it was bought by Hope Homes in 2005. In July 2006 work started on converting it to six flatted dwellings with two blocks of six flats in the playground.

The House with the Green Shutters – before it had green shutters – shortly before the First World War when it was owned by Mrs. Annie Simpson, widow of the Cumnock contractor, Alexander Simpson and occupied by Elspeth Muirhead also a widow, who died in 1946 aged 88 years. The house to the right was home to the molecatcher William Buck (1844-1935).

On 1st November 1919 the bronze plaque made by the Coylton-born artist and sculptor, Robert Bryden (1865-1939) and commemorating the birthplace of George Douglas Brown was unveiled. His birth certificate gives no address for his place of birth, merely Ochiltree. The individuals cannot be individually identified, but the group includes: Mr. Duncan Mackay, master of modern languages at Ayr Academy, who had initiated the plan; Mr. D. E. Edward of Ayr's Carnegie Library; Mr. Andrew Melrose (1860-1928), publisher of *The House with the Green Shutters,* and the prominent stationer and editor, Sir Howard Handley Spicer (1872-1926). The company afterwards adjourned to the school for an afternoon of speeches.

Main Street, from 'The House with the Green Shutters', as it runs west towards the Convalescent Home and beyond, in the early 1920s.

Born in the village on 26th January 1869, the novelist George Douglas Brown (1869-1902) put Ochiltree (or *Barbie*) on the map, with his novel *The House with the Green Shutters*. His birth certificate shows he was the illegitimate son of Sarah Gammell [sic], a dairymaid, but he was registered with the full name of his father, who farmed Drumsmudden. His education at Ayr Academy was sponsored, and he studied Classics at Glasgow University, graduating in 1890. Further studies at Balliol College, Oxford were interrupted by the illness and death of his mother, whom he nursed through her last days in May 1895. Working in London as a journalist, he contributed to *Blackwood's Magazine* and *Sandow's Magazine of Physical Culture* (a monthly journal, established in 1898 by the Prussian, Friederich Wilhelm Muller, alias Eugen Sandow (1867-1928) 'the Father of Bodybuilding'), before his first book *Love and a Sword* was published in 1899, under the pseudonym Kennedy King. It was a moderate success. In 1900 he started work on *The House with the Green Shutters* whilst living with his publisher, Andrew Melrose, at Hornsey in the now London Borough of Haringey. The book was a universal success, and he had started a second novel, *The Incompatibles*, when he died of pneumonia on 28th August 1902. His body was carried from London by train and taken to the home of his fiancé, Miss Elizabeth Smith McLennan, 'Newhall', Sydenham Road, Dowanhill, Glasgow. Her Coylton-born father, James McLennan (1839-1899), had been a successful wine and spirit merchant in the city. Brown was buried at Ayr Cemetery, Miss McLennan later erecting his headstone. The stone also carries the inscription – 'and his mother, who died 13th May 1895, aged 62 years'. Her death certificate, signed, G D Brown (son, present), records her as Sarah Gemmell Hare, aged 60 years, unmarried and living at Crofthead, Ayr.

The north side of Main Street, around 1909, when Joseph Smith was the licence holder of the Crown Inn. Over time the scene has become a good deal tidier, with clear footpaths and lined roads, but perhaps at the expense of character and interest.

Main Street, with the Barony Power Station and the colliery 'A' frame on the horizon, around 1956. On the right, beyond the demolition, was Agnes Davidson McIlwraith's shop. She later emigrated to Canada where she died, leaving a bequest to Auchinleck Academy. Her successor was John Smith, who moved the business across to the Crown Buildings and, in January 1963, sold it to Jim Brown.

The house in the centre of this 1899 photograph, stood on the north side of Main Street, and belonged to Sarah Morton, the draper, but was divided between herself and a drainer, James Service. The whitewashed, thatched, double cottage to the right was later demolished and in its place rose the Crown Buildings.

The top of the village around 1904 with the roofless ruin which Helen Holmes (nee Reid) of the Crown Inn, had demolished to erect the Crown Buildings.

The Crown Buildings were completed around 1905-1906 and subsequently the four properties were tenanted by William Barr, William Weir, Robert Service and a widow, Mrs. Jemima Mills.

Ayr and District Sick Nursing Association's Gallowlea Convalescent Home was at the top of Main Street and is seen here around 1910. A nurse (probably 21 year old assistant matron Maud Elizabeth Perry, a native of Ayr) stands with three visitors. The original house, Gallowlea Cottage, was built in the 1850s by the quarryman and mason Andrew Murdoch – 'the strongest man in Ayrshire' – and named after the Gallowlea Well, then situated on the rising ground behind. One of his sons, Alexander, penned the book *Ochiltree – Its History and Reminiscences*. In 1881 Murdoch sold the property to Mrs. Flora Campbell Whiteside, wife of Ayr solicitor George Charles Shaw, who converted it to a convalescent home. The 1911 census shows Elizabeth Morton as the matron, her assistant Maud Perry, two maids, a gardener and seven patients. She died in the home in 1915, aged 55 years. Sustained by donations and bequests, the home aided the recovery of ex-hospital patients with a healthy diet and the fresh, bracing, air above Ochiltree.

In this photograph of the Head Inn on Burnock Street the presence of the stagecoach suggests a much earlier period than the tarmacadamed road surface suggests (Ayr County Council tarred the Ayr to Cumnock road in 1925). The building was owned by John Jamieson Probert, with his son William running the pub and the hotel. The lion atop the entrance porch to the hotel disappeared when the porch was demolished in the 1940s, and is last remembered in the garden of Mrs. Mary Kay, the beadle, who lived in the last house before the church in Main Street.

Adam Wilson Montgomery (back row, centre) and Hugh Brown (back row, right) with fellow soldiers, outside Cumnock Parish Church on Sunday, 21st January 1900, following a "War Service", by the Rev. J. Spence Robertson, to mark their departure (on 23rd February) for South Africa and the Boer War. The *Cumnock Express* newspaper published the photograph (by Wilhelm Hess of Ayr and Cumnock) in a booklet to mark the event, naming the men (all who would serve with the Imperial Yeomanry except H. Murdoch and D. McTear). *Front row* (*left to right*): David McLanachan, James Murray, William McLanachan, Capt. John D. Boswell, John Macartney, James Sloan, James MacDonald. *Middle row*: William McMillan, H Murdoch, James Armstrong, William Montgomery, D. Tear, William Bruges. *Back row*: William J. G. Ogilvie, Thomas Meikle, Adam Wilson Montgomery, James Park, Hugh Brown.

This 1890s photograph of Mill Street (by Andrew Miller of the Cumnock Studio, Barrhill Road, Cumnock), looks to the Cross, with the shoemaker James Colville (in the white apron) outside his premises. Mill place was built when the buildings on the left were demolished. The cottage on the immediate right was Lady Glencairn's school. From around 1789, Elizabeth, Countess Dowager of Glencairn (1725-1801) rented it from John Samson to serve as a school for girls from five years of age. Believing that mere book learning did not prepare the girls for a life of happy domesticity, they were taught the basic skills of cooking, household management and, spinning, which financed the project. Her Ladyship was then living in Edinburgh and the Rev. David Grant managed the school's affairs.

The mill dam on the Lugar diverted water into the mill lade (out of picture to the left) which served the grain mill and the sawmill. In the background is the bridge carrying the old road to Auchinleck. In the last days of 1878 melting snows brought a flood which swept away the dam, bringing the mills to a standstill. In his book, *Ochiltree – Its History and Reminiscences*, Alexander Murdoch writes that a stone 'hump-backed' bridge replaced a wooden one in 1819, which, in turn, was replaced by the two arch one seen here. His father, the mason Andrew Murdoch of Gallowlea Cottage, started the work in early 1867 but, at the end of July, with the second arch nearing completion, another flood carried away its supports, bringing it down with 'a prodigious crash'.

The village from the north east across the Lugar Bridge, in the foreground. Despite the opening of the new bridge in 1962, the old bridge lives on unaware of the number of decisions and counter-decisions regarding its future. In 1991 renovation costs would have been £33,750. Today (2012) it would be £100,000. Perhaps, in due course, the river will decide, repeating the 'prodigious crash' of 1867.

In June 1960, John Maclay, Secretary of State for Scotland confirmed the 'County of Ayr (Lugar Bridge, Ochiltree) (Restrictions on Driving) Order', restricting the use of the 'old' bridge to vehicles under 12 tons, whilst the county council carried out urgent repairs. However, it was evident that a new bridge was needed and in February 1961 Murdoch MacKenzie Ltd. of Motherwell won the contract at a price of £59,694.

Work began on the bridge and the new road out of the village (cutting through the grounds of Ochiltree House) on Tuesday 4th April 1961, the contractor promising to complete the work in twelve months. This upstream view shows the dam, with the village to the right. With a span of 104 feet, the bridge had six, seven feet deep, steel plate girders (from P. & W. McLellan's Clutha Iron Works, Glasgow), 11 feet above normal river level, with an eight inch reinforced concrete deck surfaced with tar macadam. The 24 feet wide carriageway was flanked by six feet wide footpaths.

On Wednesday, 11th April 1962, the bridge opened to traffic without ceremony. There were no speeches, no ribbon cutting, no plaque unveiling – merely the removal of the barricades and diversion signs. This, however, left Ayr County Council with the problem of the old bridge, a problem passed to Cumnock and Doon Valley District Council and, in 1995, to East Ayrshire Council. In 1991 demolition was proposed, then abandoned. In 1999 it was designated a Class B listed structure with an estimated price of £100,000 on the required renovation work. An inspection in September 2011 found it in a neglected state, with trees and large saplings growing from the masonry. Watch this space.

Sawyer Charles McIntyre (1851-1928) and his sister Margaret (1839-1930), stooped by the doorway to the left, at the Sawmill in the early 1920s. A journeyman joiner, Charles continued the work at the mill following the death of their father, James, in 1885, aged 75 years. The mill appears to have been rebuilt in 1857 for Thomas Cuthbert (1793-1870) of Burnockholm, deriving its power from the lade previously cut for the grain mill. By 1930 it was occupied, and operated, by the joiner Hugh Morton, and he worked it until about 1980. In the 1950s the sawmill was partly demolished and the upper half rebuilt in brick as a 'modern' bungalow type house. Following Morton's death, the sawmill and sawmill house were sold in 1991 and the workshops were subsequently converted to dwelling house also, although the inner gearing was kept and incorporated as a feature.

The north side of the sawmill with its low breast, 12 feet diameter, six spoke, water wheel, driven by the lade as it flowed from the left. Prior to being a sawmill, this was a lint mill and a waulkmill. It was probably built as such with government assistance in the eighteenth century. 'Reid the Dyer' occupied the property until he died in 1817 aged 60 years old and the adjacent woodland on the bank is still known as the 'Dyester's Wood'. The mill wheel is thought to be the work of the millwright George McCartney of Cumnock.

The interior of the sawmill, photographed in 1991, with its moving table saw bench and drive belts. The increasing availability of circular saws and benches, such as these, from the 1850s brought the rapid decline of the heavy work of the sawpit.

THE MILL OCHILTREE

The present Ochiltree Mill, with its 32 acres of land, dates from the early nineteenth century and at that time was part of Carston Farm. The farm was bought by Andrew Paterson, born a farmer's son at Dalleagles, New Cumnock in 1803. He was a land surveyor, and Provost of Ayr between 1861 and 1863. Following his death in 1876 his estate was administered by trustees, with David Murdoch running the grain mill (later bought by McGill & Smith, the grain merchants of Ayr) and Charles McIntyre at the sawmill. It is said to have been a good example of a rural meal mill, its low-breast water-wheel driving four or five pairs of millstones. It's thought though that there has been a mill on or in the vicinity of this site from early times, possibly the twelfth century.

In the 1930s Langholm Farm would have produced three or four 10 gallon cans of milk daily, and to ease its collection this suspension bridge over the Lugar superceded the stepping stones (the tanker was some decades away) and relieved the lorry driver of the tortuous route through Auchinleck estate. From 1936 the milk was taken to Mauchline Creamery for the production of cream, butter and cheese.

Joseph McGovern, 'Wee Joe', an itinerant farm worker, with a young Clydesdale horse, possibly, at Langholm Farm in the 1920s. Born at 151 Sword Street (long since demolished), Glasgow in 1890, he was introduced to Ayrshire with a 'holiday' at Glasgow Corporation's home in Maybole in spring, 1901. He returned to the county in the early 1920s, working on farms around Ochiltree, and by the start of the Second World War was living in the disused Free Church. Joe died at Ayr's Heathfield Hospital, in November 1968, of a cerebral thrombosis and hypothermia, when his address was given as the Trades Hotel, a model lodging house, at 20 York Street, Ayr.

Burnockholm, Ochiltree.

This view looks east from the lands of Burnockholm, with the Burnock Water winding past to join the Lugar at Ochiltree House – just visible through the trees. Burnock Street, with the 1908 built houses on its left, runs down to the new bridge and the road to Cumnock. The roofless cottage shows the road line to the old bridge. South of the bridge is Burnockholm House. Although it appears from the road as a single storey house, this view shows the full extent of its accommodation. Little is remembered of the football pitch in the foreground. It has been suggested that the village was too small to form a team – or perhaps 'Ochiltree United' players made their way along Barony Road on Saturday afternoons.

The single span Old Burnock Bridge, photographed around 1904 when a ruin, with its successor, behind, carrying the Ayr to Cumnock road. Continuing under the bridges, the Burnock Water sweeps around the grounds of Ochiltree House before joining the Lugar Water. No dates could be found by the author for the building of either bridge but the older one, its stones now strewn by the flow of the river, does not appear on James Thomson's *Atlas of Scotland*, surveyed in 1832.

The Glasgow & South Western Railway Company's station for Ochiltree, around 1910, with the line from Ayr running under the bridge towards Muirkirk and on to Douglas in Lanarkshire. Legislation for the line was passed in November 1864 and opened, for goods traffic (mainly coal to the port of Ayr), on 11th June 1872. The passenger service between Ayr and Muirkirk commenced on Monday 1st July, with two services per day, out of Ayr (10 a.m. and 5.45 p.m.) and from Muirkirk at 8 a.m. and 3.45 p.m., with a journey time of one and a quarter hours. In September 1922 Ochiltree was judged one of the Glasgow and South Western Railway's best kept stations, earning station master John B Campbell a prize of £5. The service was lost with the closure of the line on 10th September 1951. The track is long gone, but the station building survives.

The summer camp of the South Scottish Infantry Brigade (Territorial Army) at Auchencloich Farm in the summer of 1912. It ran over two weeks, with the 5th Battalions of the Royal Scots Fusiliers (commanded by Lt. Col. J. B. Pollok-McCall, who had served in the Boer War) and the Kings Own Scottish Borderers (commanded by Colonel J. F. Erskine) encamped from the 13th July, followed by the 4th battalions of each regiment the following week. Over 2,000 men attended, and the Glasgow and South Western Railway built a spur from the Ayr to Cumnock line to serve the camp. Over the fortnight 12,000 men were under canvas in Ayrshire – 3,884 at Doonfoot in Ayr, 3,640 at Gailes near Irvine and 2,800 at Muirend in Troon. With only two years until the outbreak of the First World War many of the names on the camp muster rolls would in time be appearing on granite memorials.

Left: This silver medal was won by Thomas Lindsay (1829-1915) of *Rudston - For The Best Pair 2 Year Old Queys* at Ochiltree Farmers' Society Show in 1888. However, it remains with the show committee, the engraver having misspelled the farm name *Reidston*. The society was founded in 1846, as were many around the country at this time with the aim of improving both farming methods and dairy stock. The following year they held their first show – to be held annually on the Wednesday nearest to the 15th of May. Over the years, the range of classes increased, from the initial ploughing competition and cattle, to include poultry, collie dogs and, in 1947 with the formation of a ladies committee, baking and handicrafts.

Above: Patrons of The Commercial Inn, Mill Street, photographed on their outing to the village of Leadhills in Lanarkshire in the summer of 1958. The, crouched, front row consists of: George Hendry, Robert Fleming, Tom Fleming, Sid Foulds, Ned McCrorie, Alex McCrorie, Joe Nutt, J Hazlett (sitting on the ball), John Brown, George Cunningham, Jimmy Hendry, Norman Wyllie, Tom Hendry, James Faulds (Sid's son), Willie McCrorie and Tom Griffin. Fifth from the left, of those standing, is Morton, proprietor of the pub, who organised the annual outings. The previous year they had visited the Daljarrock Inn and the following summer it would be Peebles. Do you recognise anyone?

Ochiltree House (where John Knox was married)

The coalmaster James Angus (1864-1902) and his family and servants outside Ochiltree House, which he rented from the Marquis of Bute, around 1900. The house had four public rooms, seven bedrooms, two dressing rooms, three servants' bedrooms, a three stall stable, and a coachman's house, on a four acre policy, and dated from the 1680s. The original fortified house, in which John Knox married Margaret Stewart, daughter of Andrew, 2nd Lord Stuart of Ochiltree in 1564, was lost to a fire and this house built to replace it – the ruins of the old house survived in the garden into the 20th century. It had a succession of tenants, and was the parish manse in the 1790s, but worsening decay led to its demolition in March 1952. The name lives on with a house built on the site in 1972.

The bases of the Barony Power Station cooling towers in October 1955. In June 1953 approval for its building, at a cost of £4,000,000, was granted by Geoffrey Lloyd, Minister of Fuel and Power, and work began in the July. In 1956, peat was considered as a fuel – the Barony could have been supplied from Airds Moss, but after experiments at Bonnybridge Power Station (demolished 1976) in Stirlingshire, slurry won the day, and by 1963 the Barony was consuming 336,000 tons per annum.

The towers photographed from the south west in December 1955. The main contractor was John Laing & Son of Glasgow, with Bierrum & Partners, founded by Hans Bierrum in 1927, of Harrow in Middlesex, responsible for the towers. Other contractors were: Aird, Walker and Ralston, Kilmarnock, for the electrical, lighting and power installation; Babcock and Wilcox, boiler plant equipment; The Coppee Company of London for the coal preparation plant and Wallacetown Engineering Company of Ayr for the control gear.

The completed power station, with the furnaces burning, in the summer of 1958 with Barony Road in the foreground and Ochiltree on the horizon to the right. It was commissioned on 11th October 1957 by John S. Maclay, Secretary of State for Scotland (1957-1961), and future Viscount Muirshiel of Kilmalcolm, on behalf of the South of Scotland Electricity Board.

Right: The pump house and the cooling tower pond, photographed on 17 July 1957. Standing on a 137 feet diameter base, the 210 feet high towers terminated with a 62 feet wide top rim. The hyperbolic shell induced a draught of air to enter the tower at the base, where steam from the system was sprayed onto timber lathes, falling as droplets of water into the pond from where they returned to the boilers to become the steam which drove the turbines. The cycle used approximately one million gallons of water per hour.

Overleaf: The cooling tower pond with the spiral stairway to the inspection gallery, with the tree-lined Barony Road in the background.

In November 1981, with diminishing sources of slurry, and the Barony's nominal output of 60 megawatts dwarfed by the 600 megawatt output of the nuclear power station at Hunterston, the South of Scotland Electricity Board decided that it would close in March 1983. The workforce of 147 industrial and 26 non-industrial employees would be re-deployed or re-trained. The date of demolition was set for Sunday 20th November 1983, and W. J. & D. (Demolitions) Ltd. of Glasgow were commissioned to bring down the towers by controlled explosions. Barony Road was closed to traffic from 11.00 a.m. and the previously drilled holes around the base of each tower filled with 20 lbs of gelignite. At 1.00 p.m. the giant cruet set, 'puffed, heaved and twisted before collapsing in a cloud of dust'.

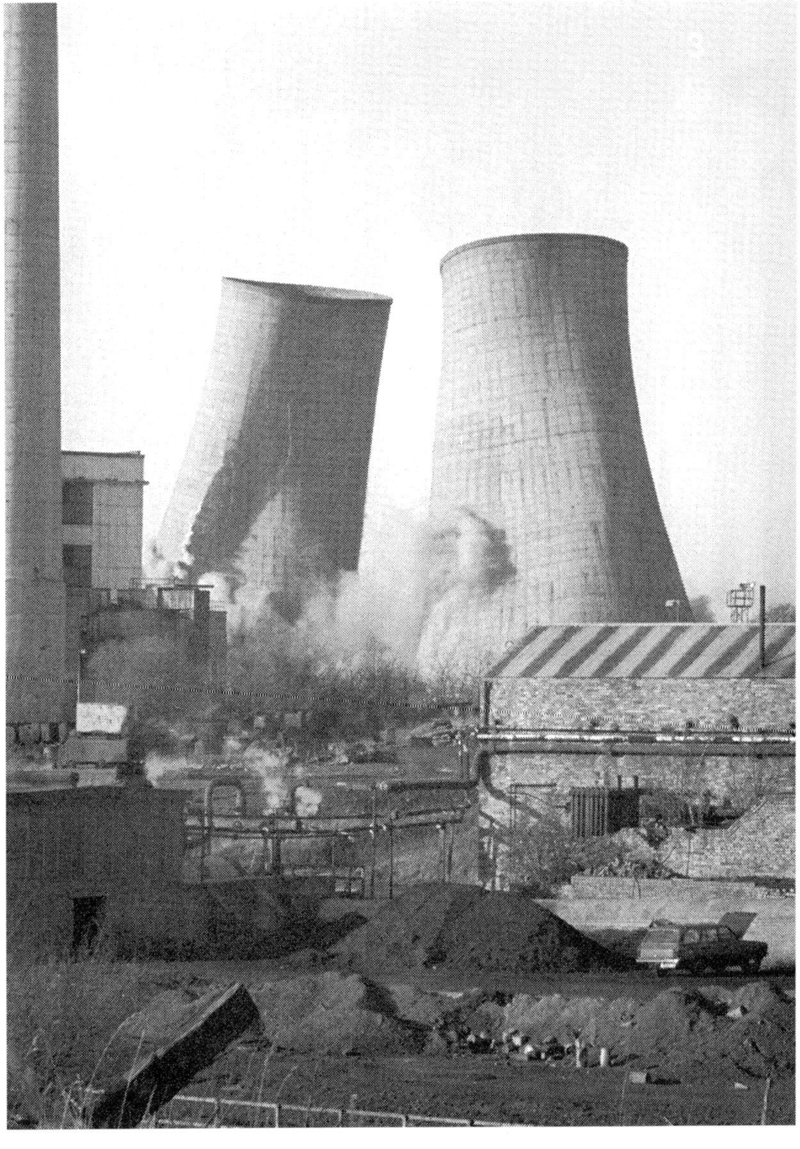

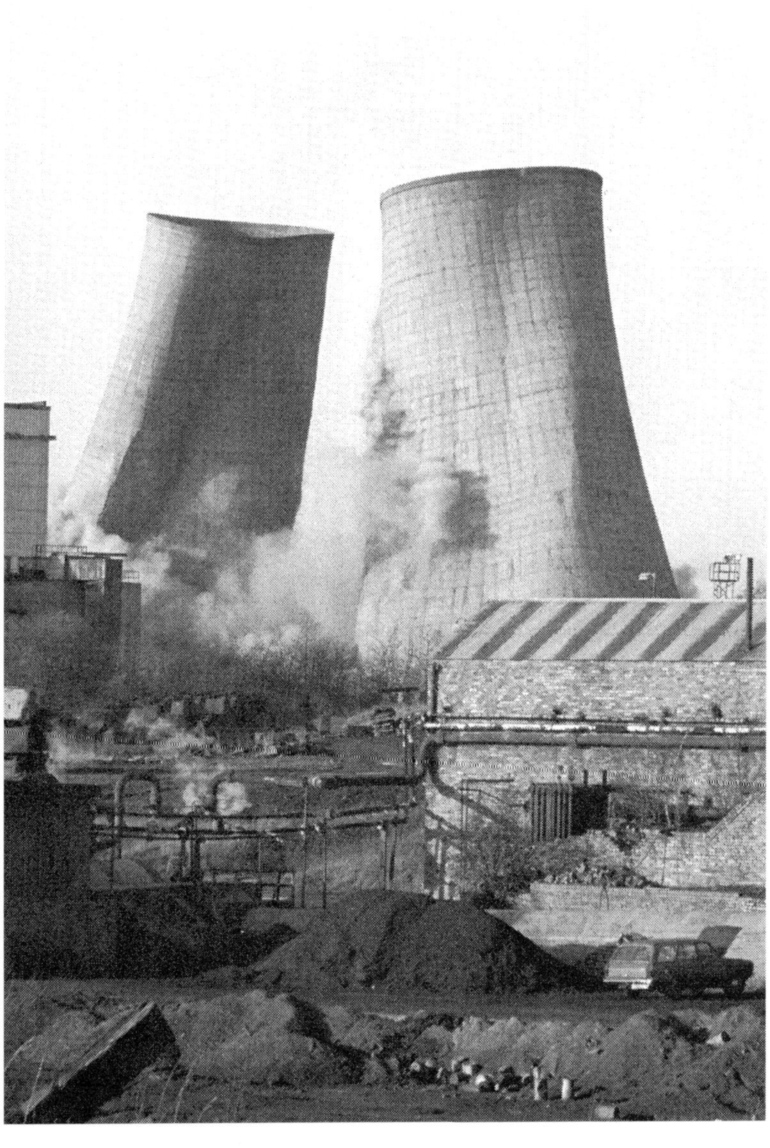

55

56